Supernatural

Alan Leonhardt

Published by Lionheart Publications,
   a division of Lionheart Ministries
1600 W. State Rd
Hastings, MI 49058
alanleonhardt@gmail.com

Credits:
Cover design, editing, and interior design by Kathy Mayo
Cover photo taken by author, Alan Leonhardt:
        Lake Michigan and North Breakwater Lighthouse
        in Ludington, MI

ISBNs: 978-1-7348354-4-1 (printed)
        978-1-7348354-5-8 (ebook)
First edition: January 2021
Printed in the United States of America

Previous Books by Alan Leonhardt

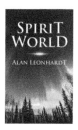

Spirit World, 2019

There is a deep spiritual side to the Christian experience. In this book, Dr Leonhardt relates his own personal journey with dreams, visions, hearing from God, speaking in tongues, and other powerful gifts of the Holy Spirit.

Pathway to Promotion, 2020

God has a destiny for every believer. He wants to bless you exceedingly, abundantly and above your wildest dreams. As we cooperate with God's principles for advancement, we will break out of a mediocre Christian life and find the Pathway to Promotion.

Supernatural Joy, 2020

How is your joy level? Jesus said, "Ask that your Joy may be full" (John 16:24). In this 21-day devotional, you will learn how to access the "Supernatural Joy" of God. Learn what it means to hope and have a positive expectation of your future.

Dedication

I want to dedicate all my books to my wife Nicole, my four beautiful daughters, and the next generation.

One generation shall praise Your works to another, And shall declare Your mighty acts.
~ Psalm 145:4

We have an obligation to pass on our wisdom and experience to the next generation. My biggest inspirations are my children. I want my ceiling in life to be their starting place and platform.

If we are wise, we will admit that we all stand on the shoulders of great men and women who have mentored us with the sacrifice of their lives. If someone can glean any good thing from my books that will help establish them and give them greater endurance to finish their race, then I will have done my job.

Contents

What is God's Peace?

Accessing God's Supernatural Peace

Being at Peace with Yourself and Others

Introduction

Anxiety in the heart of man causes depression,
but a good word makes it glad.
~ Proverbs 12:25

If there was ever a time when people needed the supernatural peace and joy that are found in Christ, it's now. Not only does the world need it, but Christians need to access the peace of the Holy Spirit like never before. Observe the following quote:

> *"Anxiety disorders are the most common mental illness in the U.S., affecting 40 million adults in the United States age 18 and older, or 18.1% of the population every year. Anxiety disorders are highly treatable, yet only 36.9% of those suffering receive treatment." (Anxiety and Depression Association of America, www.adaa.org)*

The cure will always be the same; Jesus. The treatment for anxiety is a good word. This devotional offers that good word. Spirit, mind, and heart need to come into alignment with the Word of God and the Spirit of God. If I can get people to sit under the Word of God, and they allow it to permeate their souls, it will grow mightily and prevail over anxiety. The Word of God is the incorruptible seed that will cure anxiety, phobias, depression, and every other "mental disorder" known to man. One of my favorite verses in the Gospels is in reference to the time when the man tormented with demons is delivered by Jesus, and then he sits at Jesus' feet in his right mind.

Then they came to Jesus, and saw the one who had been
demon-possessed and had the legion, sitting and clothed and
in his right mind. *And they were afraid.*
~ Mark 5:15

At what point did the church lose its healing virtue? Jesus is a holistic healer. He heals body, soul, and spirit. There is hope for those who need the supernatural peace of Almighty God. Having a healthy soul (mind and emotional makeup) is the key to physical healing and prosperity.

[2] Beloved, I pray that you may prosper in all things and be in
*health, **just as your soul prospers.** [3] For I rejoiced greatly*
*when brethren came and testified of **the truth that is in***
***you,** just **as you walk in the truth.** [4] I have no greater joy*
than to hear that my children walk in truth.
~ III John 1:2-4

Prospering in all things and being in heath is dependent on the prosperity of the soul. How does the soul prosper? By knowing the truth and walking it out. It's time to saturate yourself in the healing Word of God. It's time to partner with the Holy Spirit to obtain freedom; a supernatural peace that surpasses human comprehension.

Let our journey into the supernatural peace of God begin.

Pastor Alan Leonhardt D.Th

What is
God's Peace?

*If worry is the symptom, then Doctor Jesus
gives you the prescription of Matthew 6:25-34.*

*As you are faithful to take your
vitamin-rich faith supplement every day,
your faith will be strengthened.
Worry will be overtaken by peace.
Doubt and fear will be conquered
by faith and trust.*
~ Alan Leonhardt

Day 1

Speak Shalom

Behold, on the mountains the feet of him who brings
*good tidings, who proclaims **peace!***
~ Nahum 1:15a

The scriptures show that God has given Christians the authority to speak and declare peace.

Years ago, I was in a Christian rock band and one particular gig was on a Lake Michigan beach. It was the fourth of July and the beach was packed. Hundreds of people were lounging on beach blankets and folding chairs waiting for the show to begin. We knew that this was going to be a great opportunity to share our music and the gospel.

As we looked out over Lake Michigan, we could see a storm rolling toward us from the west. We quickly gathered in a circle behind the stage and began to pray. We took authority over the storm and commanded that it would *not* rain on that beach. And then an amazing thing happened! As we played our music and gave testimonies about what Jesus had done in our lives, the storm parted into two parts; one half went around us to the north, and the other half went around us to the south. Nothing but sunny skies were left on that beach where we were performing.

Our assignment to preach the gospel to the people on that beach was threatened by a Lake Michigan squall. Jesus prayed the same way when a storm threatened His assignment to go to the other side of a lake to minister to a demonized man; He rose up and spoke PEACE to that storm:

> *Then He arose and rebuked the wind, and said to the sea,* **"Peace, be still!"** *And the wind ceased and there was a great calm.*
> *~ Mark 4:39*

There are 3 types of storms:

1. **Storms of correction** (see Jonah 1): The story of Jonah is an example of a storm of correction. If we repent and turn to God, He will deliver us from the corrective tempest.

2. **Random storms of life** (see Matthew 7:24-29): When you build your house on the rock (teachings) of Christ, you will stand through the random storms of life. We live in a sinful world; bad things can happen to good people, but God can sustain and deliver us(see Psalm 34:6, Romans 8:18, 28).

3. **Storms of opposition** (see Mark 4:39): We are to take authority over the storms of opposition by speaking peace to them. The demonic hordes of hell will do anything to stop you from advancing the kingdom of God. However, Jesus has given us authority over devils (see Luke 10:17-20) and we can overcome all the power of the enemy.

The Old Testament word for peace is "shalom" (Strong's #7965). It not only means peace and tranquility, but also carries with it the idea of prosperity, wholeness, completeness, and well-being. In Isaiah 53:5b, the scripture states, *"The chastisement for our peace was upon Him, and by His stripes we are healed."* Jesus paid the price on the cross so that you and I could claim the shalom of God upon our lives. Through Christ, we have wholeness and peace in our spirit, soul, and bodies. When we bless others with the ancient Hebrew word, "shalom;" we are imparting peace, wholeness, and prosperity.

> *⁵But whatever house you enter, first say, 'Peace to this house.'*
> *⁶And if a son of peace is there, your peace will rest*
> *on it; if not, it will return to you.*
> *~ Luke 10:5-6*

Whenever I enter a home, I do what Jesus said to do; I speak "shalom" over that home. You have the right to speak shalom in the mighty name of Jesus. You have the power to bless and take authority over storms of opposition.

Many times, I get attacked on Saturday nights; the enemy likes to disrupt my sleep causing me to be sluggish in the pulpit on Sunday mornings. I started working on this Devotional one Saturday evening, and that night I experienced nightmares and accusations coming to my mind trying to make me feel unworthy and condemned. I heard the still small voice of the Holy Spirit say, "*Speak peace!*" I thought to myself, "It's time to use what I had written about." I rose up and declared PEACE over my sleep, over my bedroom and home, and over my wife. The shalom of God came upon me and I slept like a baby the rest of the night.

Speak Shalom!

Day 2

The Way of Peace

*To give light to those who sit in darkness and the shadow
of death, to guide our feet into the way of **peace**.*
~ Luke 1:79

The Greek word in the New Testament for peace is "Eirene" (Strong's #1515). This word means tranquility, calmness, state of rest, and absence of strife; but it also means perfect well-being. It's the peace provided to the followers of Jesus. It is the fruit of the Holy Spirit's work in our lives (see Galatians 5:22). Fruit needs to be cultivated; good fruit does not always reveal itself right away. God wants to guide us into the way of peace. He wants to develop in us a lifestyle of experiencing His supernatural peace.

Mark the blameless man, and observe the upright;
For the future of that man is peace.
~ Psalm 37:37

When I first came to the Lord, I did not always experience supernatural peace, it would come and go; I was on an emotional rollercoaster ride. Anxiety attacks were not uncommon. Thank God for the Holy Ghost, and thank God for the gift of praying in tongues.

One evening I was discouraged by my circumstances in life. Some of my High School friends were graduating from college and beginning to prosper. Friends who weren't serving the Lord seemed to have it all together. I was making the dangerous mistake of comparing myself with others (see I Corinthians 10:12).

The Holy Spirit is the great teacher and He is guiding you and me into all truth (see John 16:13). He is trying to change our way of thinking so that we can maintain the peace of Christ in our lives. He led me to Psalm 37:37 and assured me that my end would be peace. The more established and grounded you become in your faith, the more peace you will access. This is a lifelong process. Although when *I* came to Christ, there was an immediate peace; I was safe under the protection of God. Maintaining that peace was something that also needed to be cultivated. We must turn over the hard, dry, uncultivated soil of our hearts and receive, with humility, the incorruptible seed of God's Word (see I Peter 1:23, James 1:21). The Word must be watered by staying connected to a community of believers. The Word must receive the sunlight of hearing anointed Bible teachers teach. Our root system must go down deep into the soil of God's love and faithfulness.

²But his delight is in the law of the Lord, and in His law he meditates day and night. ³He shall be like a tree planted by the rivers of water, that brings forth its fruit in its season, whose leaf also shall not wither; and whatever he does shall prosper.
~ Psalm 1:2-3

Your end will also be peace; God is guiding you into a harvest of Eirene. The Word of God will grow mightily and prevail over doubt and unbelief. The Word of God will prevail over fear and anxiety.

Declare and pray this:
I shall not die, but live, and declare the works of the Lord (Psalm 118:17). Thank You Lord for Your wonderful peace. I receive Your leading and guidance into my life. Lead me into the way of peace.
In Jesus' name, Amen

Day 3

Let God's Peace Rule

*[15]And let the **peace of God rule in your hearts,** to which also you were called in one body; and be thankful. [16]Let the word of Christ dwell in you richly in all wisdom, teaching and admonishing one another in psalms and hymns and spiritual songs, singing with grace in your hearts to the Lord.*
~ Colossians 3:15-16

Let the peace of Christ (the inner calm of one who walks daily with Him) be the controlling factor in your hearts (deciding and settling questions that arise). To this peace indeed you were called as members in one body (of believers). And be thankful (to God always) (Colossians 3:15).

The peace of God can lead you; this is one of the main ways that God speaks to your heart. When you are faced with major decisions, you can check your heart for God's peace. His peace will lead you and will be an umpire helping you to make some hard calls.

*For you shall go out with joy, and **be led out with peace**; the mountains and the hills shall break forth into singing before you, and all the trees of the field shall clap their hands.*
~ Isaiah 55:12

*Depart from evil and do good; **Seek peace and pursue it.***
~ Psalm 34:14

A friend asked me to pray with him about buying some property in front of a cinema plex on which he wanted to build a putt-putt golf course. We both prayed for a week and I told him I had total peace about it. He said that was confirmation, and so he built the putt-putt and it prospered.

About two years later he asked me to pray with him again about selling all his businesses and moving to Tulsa, Oklahoma. I asked him why he wanted to move to Tulsa. He told me his wife was unhappy and wanted to move there. After praying for a week, I had NO peace about him moving his family to Tulsa. In fact, it was just the opposite; I felt grieved in my spirit when I thought about him and his family moving to Tulsa. I told him that if his wife was restless and unhappy, they may need some counseling. He ignored my advice and moved to Tulsa to please his wife, and perhaps save his marriage. A year later she was having an affair and they were going through a divorce.

I am NOT saying that we need to check in with spiritual leadership every time we have a big decision. Good pastors and spiritual leadership never want folks to become codependent on them. I want folks to hear from God for themselves. As a pastor, I can only advise; I can't make anyone do anything. I generally want people to work out their OWN salvation (see Philippians 2:12-13), but if you ask me to pray with you about something, I will tell you how I think and feel about it. Sometimes I get a total blank about a situation. When that happens, the Lord is telling me that it's none of my business and He wants to speak and minister to them without my assistance. I'm fine with that because my job is to make people more dependent on God, not on me. That being said, there have been times when an intervention was needed. I generally don't like to give unsolicited advice unless the lack of peace is overwhelming.

"And let the peace of God rule in your hearts."
~ Colossians 3:15

When the Bible tells us to let the peace of God rule in our hearts, it means to let God's peace be an umpire calling the shots. There will be times when God's peace is hard to find in the cacophony of conflicting voices. When you find yourself under extreme pressure, you may feel compelled to make a quick decision. Let me just tell you this, the enemy (the demonic) *pushes* you through fear and anxiety. God *leads* us with His peace. Even if God's leading has an urgency about it, there is still a secure calm and a reassurance of His sovereign care.

*¹God is our refuge and strength, a very present help in trouble. ²**Therefore we will not fear**, even though the earth be removed, and though the mountains be carried into the midst of the sea; ³Though its waters roar and be troubled, though the mountains shake with its swelling. Selah*
~ Psalm 46:1-3

Prayer:
Heavenly Father,
Please help me discern between Your peace and the pushiness of the enemy. Please help me discern Your peace in the midst of any storm that life can throw at me. I don't want to confuse Your peace with me wanting something comfortable. I don't want to confuse me wanting to escape something difficult, from Your peace leading to face up to life's challenges. You are the strength of my life. I look to You for guidance and help. In Jesus name, Amen

The Lord is my light and my salvation; Whom shall I fear? The Lord is the strength of my life; Of whom shall I be afraid?
~ Psalm 27:1

Day 4

The God of Peace

*²³Now may the **God of peace** Himself sanctify you completely;*
and may your whole spirit, soul, and body be preserved
blameless at the coming of our Lord Jesus Christ.
*²⁴**He who calls you is faithful, who also will do it.***
~ I Thessalonians 5:23-24

In our Holy Bible, our God is called, "the God of peace." He is the fountainhead from which all true peace and tranquility flow. It makes sense that as we grow in our faith and closeness to our creator, our ability to live in the supernatural peace zone should increase.

Our God *IS* love (see I John 4:8), He's not just the God *of* love. He is the truest definition of what love is. Besides being the God of peace, He's also the God of hope (see Romans 15:13), the God of all comfort (see II Corinthians 1:3), the Father of mercies (see II Corinthians 1:3), the God of the living (see Matthew 22:32), the God of gods (see Joshua 22:22), and the God of hosts (see Psalm 69:6).

The title, "the God of hosts" is the most used name of God in the Bible. It means that He commands the vast angel armies of heaven; it is a military title. Our God is also a God of war. I can almost hear you saying in your mind, "Wait a minute, how can the God of peace also be the God of war?" Because sometimes peace can only be found on the other side of war.

*And the God of peace will crush Satan under your feet shortly.
The grace of our Lord Jesus Christ be with you. Amen.*
~ Romans 16:20

Notice that the God of peace will go to war and violently crush Satan under your feet. God is partnering with you to crush the attacks of Satan. It's YOUR feet God is using. That means you are partnering with God to overcome attacks and achieve the supernatural peace of God.

The Lord is a warrior; the Lord is his name.
~ Exodus 15:3

To quote King Arthur in the movie *First Knight*: "*There is a peace to be found on the other side of war: If that war should come, I will fight it.*"

I will train you how to fight for the peace of God; how to take every thought captive to the obedience of Christ; how to pray through to peace; and how to fight the good fight of faith. We are in partnership with God. The initial verse I shared, I Thessalonians 5:23-24, tells us about God sanctifying you completely; your whole man, your spirit, soul, and body. The word "sanctify" means "to set you apart for holy purposes." God has promised to help you in your journey. He is partnering with you to change and transform you into a holy warrior; a peace warrior. Our job is just to submit to His training; to follow Him with all our hearts and He will help us. *Do your best and God will do the rest.*

*Blessed be the Lord my Rock, Who trains my hands
for war, And my fingers for battle.*
~ Psalm 144:1

*[12]Therefore, my beloved, as you have always obeyed, not as in my presence only, but now much more in my absence, **work out your own salvation with fear and trembling;** [13]**for it is God who works in you both to will and to do for His good pleasure.**
~ Philippians 2:12-13*

Which one is it? Are we working out our own salvation, or is God working in us? It's both. It's a partnership between us and God. That being said, I don't always have enough faith in my ability to complete the job. I need God's help. I love the following verses that promise God's help and sovereign oversight in making me a better person and getting me to heaven.

*Being confident of this very thing, that He who has begun a good work in you **will complete** it until the day of Jesus Christ.*
~ Philippians 1:6

*And let the beauty of the Lord our God be upon us, and **establish** the work of our hands for us; Yes, **establish** the work of our hands.*
~ Psalm 90:17

[20]*Now may the **God of peace** who brought up our Lord Jesus from the dead, that great Shepherd of the sheep, through the blood of the everlasting covenant,* [21]***make you complete** in every good work to do His will, working in you what is well pleasing in His sight, through Jesus Christ, to whom be glory forever and ever. Amen.*
~ Hebrews 13:20-21

Prayer:
Dear Lord,
Thank You for working in me what is well-pleasing to You. I pledge to do my part in possessing Your supernatural peace, but I can't do it on my own. I have faith that You will complete that which You began in me. I love You and put my faith completely in Your loving care.
In Jesus name, Amen

Day 5

The Focused Mind

*You will keep him in perfect peace, whose mind is stayed
on You, because he trusts in You.*
~ Isaiah 26:3

What is peace of mind worth? Before we can begin to answer that question, what does peace of mind even look like? If you've never experienced a settled tranquility of mind, you would have no idea what it is. Before I was introduced to Jesus and experienced a connection with God, I had not really known *true* peace.

I don't think I would be able to survive now without trusting in God. This world is so unstable. Have you ever felt terrified and alone? Unprotected and vulnerable; totally at the mercy of malevolent forces? But then you experience the safety and protection of Almighty God; you literally can feel His covering and care.

> *⁴I sought the Lord, and He heard me, and delivered me from all my fears. ⁵They looked to Him and were radiant, and their faces were not ashamed. ⁶This poor man cried out, and the Lord heard him, and saved him out of all his troubles. ⁷The angel of the Lord encamps all around those who fear Him, and delivers them.*
> *~ Psalm 34:4-7*

Surely I have calmed and quieted my soul, Like a weaned child
with his mother; Like a weaned child is my soul within me.
~ Psalm 131:2

Whenever situations seem overwhelming, I immediately put my trust in the Lord. I say quiet prayers that go something like this: *"Lord, I don't know how You're going to work this out but I trust You. You have my good in mind. You have the good of my family in mind. You will bring some great things out of this. I trust You and I love You."*

We need to train our minds to trust God. He WILL lead us through all of life's difficulties. We can experience a peace that passes all understanding when we learn to trust in God. For every problem, there is a solution. And when you are powerless, God can work it out and lead you to victory.

*Now thanks be to God who **always leads us in triumph***
in Christ, and through us diffuses the fragrance of
His knowledge in every place.
~ II Corinthians 2:14

This verse states that God will ALWAYS lead us to victory. When you look at the Greek, 'always' means ALWAYS. There is some kind of victory to be obtained out of every tragedy. Every trial has a silver lining. This is the beauty of trusting in God and putting your mind at rest. When your mind is grounded in solid trust, you will have emotional stability.

⁵Trust in the Lord with all your heart, and lean not on your
own understanding; ⁶In all your ways acknowledge Him,
and He shall direct your paths.
~ Proverbs 3:5-6

Don't hold back trust. Don't lean on your ability to figure things out on your own. There are so many things that are beyond our comprehension.

I was asked to officiate at a funeral for a baby girl who was born with birth defects and lived only a few hours after her birth. It was painful. I had no profound encouragement for her Mom and Dad. I had no answers for this tragedy. When the miracle doesn't come, what are you left with? You must continue to believe in God's love, compassion, and comfort.

As I prepared for the funeral, I heard the Lord tell me that **"trust when you don't understand is the highest form of faith."** This goes right along with Proverbs 3:5 & 6, *"Trust in the Lord with all your heart and lean not on your own understanding."* As we trust, He will also lead us out the dark night of the soul. *"In all your ways acknowledge Him, and He shall direct your paths."*

The Bible doesn't tell you to empty your mind to obtain peace. This is eastern mysticism. The Bible tells you instead to think on the Lord and His promises. To fill your mind with hopeful prognostications, and take captive vain, hopeless thoughts of despair and failure.

> [8]*Finally, brothers and sisters, whatever is true, whatever is noble, whatever is right, whatever is pure, whatever is lovely, whatever is admirable—if anything is excellent or praiseworthy—**think about such things.** [9]Whatever you have learned or received or heard from me, or seen in me—put it into practice. **And the God of peace will be with you.***
> *~ Philippians 4:8-9 NIV*

> [4]*For the weapons of our warfare are not carnal but mighty in God for pulling down strongholds, [5]**casting down arguments** and every high thing that exalts itself against the knowledge of God, **bringing every thought into captivity to the obedience of Christ.***
> *~ II Corinthians 10:4-5*

> **Meditate on these things***; give yourself entirely to them, that your progress may be evident to all.*
> *~ I Timothy 4:15*

Do you see how the Bible doesn't tell you to empty your mind but to renew it and think faith-filled thoughts (see Romans 12:2)?

I was with a Christian friend, and I couldn't stop talking about God and the Bible. My friend said, "Is that all you think and talk about is God and the Bible?" The question took me a little off guard. In my naiveté, I thought all Christians wanted to talk about God. I responded with these scriptures:

> [5]*For those who live according to the flesh **set their minds on the things of the flesh**, but those who live according to the Spirit, the things of the Spirit. [6]For to be carnally minded is death, but **to be spiritually minded is life and peace.***
> ~ Romans 8:5-6

Prayer:
Dear Father in heaven,
I will put my trust in You. I will trust You even when I don't understand. Especially when I don't understand. Help me to keep my mind on You and Your great and precious promises. I thank You for the abundance of peace available to me as I trust in Your loving care.
In Jesus name, Amen

Day 6

Do Not Worry

*Therefore I say to you, **do not worry** about your life,*
what you will eat or what you will drink; nor about your
body, what you will put on. Is not life more than food
and the body more than clothing?
~ Matthew 6:25
(Please read till the end of the chapter, Matthew 6:25-34)

Some of us are champion worriers. We can see disaster coming 10 miles away. Imagination is not lacking as we create destructive scenarios in our heads. Worry is kin to fearfulness and fretfulness.

I was 21 when I gave my heart to the Lord and became born-again. I moved out of my parents' home and into a one-bedroom apartment. Living on your own for the first time, whether it's at college, the military, or wherever, is a bipolar event. Let me explain; although you're excited to be out on your own and ready for the great adventure, there can be bouts of anxiety. I was far enough away from home that I couldn't just bum $20 bucks from my Dad if I was in a tight spot.

When I felt overwhelmed with worry and vulnerability, I would read Matthew 6:25-34. I sometimes read it several times a day. At times, I would read it out loud. It got to the point where I could quote it. Then, something amazing happened; I stopped worrying.

The Word of God is compared to seed in the Bible (see Mark 4:13-14, I Peter 1:23). If you keep planting the seed of God's Word on the fertile soil of your heart, you WILL reap a harvest. If worry is the symptom, then Doctor Jesus gives you the prescription of Matthew 6:25-34. As you are faithful to take your vitamin-rich faith supplement every day, your faith will be strengthened. Worry will be overtaken by peace. Doubt and fear will be conquered by faith and trust.

> *But seek first the kingdom of God and His righteousness,*
> *and all these things shall be added to you.*
> *~ Matthew 6:33*

I reached an age when I decided that I wanted a wife, and the thought occurred to me to go wife hunting. I visited area churches and college campus fellowships. I had a couple of good leads that I was about to follow up on when the Holy Spirit admonished me about being self-willed. (I'm sure you've never been guilty of that.) So I applied the same Bible verses that helped me overcome worry to then finding a wife. I believed that if I simply concentrated on seeking God and being obedient to His will, He would lead me to the right woman to marry. When the Bible said to seek first the Kingdom of God and His righteousness, and *all these THINGS* would be added to you, it means **everything** we need for life and godliness will be provided in God's time (see II Peter 1:3-4). And sure enough, God led me to a Bible college where I met my wife. (This is only the short story version since this is a *daily* Devotional.)

> *But the path of the just is like the shining sun, that*
> *shines ever brighter unto the perfect day.*
> *~ Proverbs 4:18*

Follow what you know to be God's will today, and then more light will be given to you. You may not get the 20-year plan, since so much of what God wants to do with us tomorrow is dependent on our obedience today. Continue to follow the path lit up by God's Word. The Holy Spirit will only lead in unity with the written Word of God.

> *Your word is a lamp to my feet and a light to my path.*
> *~ Psalm 119:105*

Prayer:
Thank You, Father.
I commit today to plant the Word of God in my heart. I will not worry. I will not fear, for You have promised to take care of me and lead me in Your path. If worry and anxiety try to attack my peace, I will read Matthew 6:25-34. I commit to growing my trust and dependence on You.
In the name of Jesus, I pray, Amen.

Day 7

Peace with God

*Therefore, having been justified by faith, we have peace
with God through our Lord Jesus Christ.*
~ Romans 5:1

Have you made your peace with God? There was a time when I was in denial. At that time I would have answered yes to that question, but I would have been lying to myself. My relationship with God was surface at best.

I was 16 years old and washing dishes at a restaurant. One day, management partnered me up with a 'Jesus freak'. This guy carried a little pocket New Testament with the Psalms and Proverbs in his back pocket. Who does that? I'll tell you who, a hippy Jesus freak. He started on me with his salvation questions, "Have you been born again?" "If you were to die today, do you know if you would go to heaven?" "Do you have peace with God?" Etcetera, etcetera, etcetera...

I became his personal soul-winning project. I would ask evasive questions like, "What happened to the dinosaurs?" "Did the sons of Adam have to marry their sisters?" "If the pygmy people in Africa never hear the gospel will they go to hell?" You know, all the types of questions that would help me avoid talking about my sin and conviction before God.

Then one day, my hippy freak friend decided to switch tactics on me. He came directly at me with a verse in the book of Revelation:

15I know your works, that you are neither cold nor hot.
I could wish you were cold or hot. 16So then, because
you are lukewarm, and neither cold nor hot,
I will vomit you out of My mouth.
~ Revelation 3:15-16

He told me that if I'm not fully committed to Christ then I'm on the fence; I'm lukewarm and Jesus will puke me out of His mouth, and I will not make it to heaven. He also told me that when Jesus called Peter to follow Him, Peter left all and followed Him. Then he asked, "What have you given up to follow Jesus?" Wow! I was gut-punched. I was doing my best to hide my conviction.

So when they had brought their boats to land,
they forsook all and followed Him.
~ Luke 5:11

23Then He said to them all, "If anyone desires to come after
Me, let him deny himself, and take up his cross daily, and follow
Me. 24For whoever desires to save his life will lose it,
but whoever loses his life for My sake will save it. 25For
what profit is it to a man if he gains the whole world,
and is himself destroyed or lost?"
~ Luke 9:23-25

So, let me ask *you* my opening question again; have you made your peace with God? Nothing but full surrender will do. You must also surrender your anger and fear, even if your anger is against God Himself. To have true peace we must surrender our demand for all the answers. Some things are beyond our ability to comprehend on this side of heaven.

*5**Trust** in the Lord with all your heart, and **lean not on your***
***own understanding**; 6In all your ways acknowledge Him,*
and He shall direct your paths.
~ Proverbs 3:5-6

Trust Him and make your peace right now.

Prayer:
Dear Father in heaven,
Forgive me for my sins. Forgive me for my anger with
You. I choose to trust You with my whole heart. I will
follow You, Jesus. I believe You died for my sins. You died
for my shame. Take this shame, all of it. I can't carry it
anymore. I believe that You rose from the dead so that
I could have eternal life. Come into my life and heart. I
receive You as Lord and savior today.
In Jesus' name, Amen

Now that you have made your peace with God, feel the relief and safety of His full covering and protection over your life. Here are some Bible verses that will assure you of your new life in Christ.

Therefore, if anyone is in Christ, he is a new creation; old
things have passed away; behold, all things have become new.
~ II Corinthians 5:17

But as many as received Him, to them He gave the right to
become children of God, to those who believe in His name.
~ John 1:12

If you said that prayer and meant it, you can now have access and enjoy true peace. Lay your burdens down. Find a church that preaches Jesus and grow in your faith.

Accessing God's Supernatural Peace

*It is very important that we become
people of faith and vision, and that
we grab a hold of what God is
saying in every circumstance.
Your peace depends on knowing
the report of the Lord,
"Do not be afraid; only believe."
~ Alan Leonhardt*

Day 8

Do not be Afraid, Only Believe

³⁵While He was still speaking, some came from the ruler of the synagogue's house who said, "Your daughter is dead. Why trouble the Teacher any further?" ³⁶As soon as Jesus heard the word that was spoken, He said to the ruler of the synagogue, "Do not be afraid; only believe."
~ Mark 5:35-36

In these verses, there are 2 reports. The first is the report of the world, or maybe even well-meaning people; it's a report of death. A report that sucks the hope right out of the room. While we live in this world there will always be reports that *do not factor in the promises of God.*

The second report is the report of the Lord. *"Do not be afraid; only believe."* The Lord's report to not be afraid is found many times in the Bible. The encouragement, and sometimes the command, to not be afraid, or *fear not*, is found 365 times in the Bible; once for every day of the year. God's word will oftentimes encourage us to look beyond the things we can see with the eye. We hear and see the natural, hopeless report of the world, but what does the Lord say? You can't just see and hear what is in the natural, you must develop spiritual discernment. You CAN see and hear beyond this plane of existence.

There are SO many Biblical examples of this. If you want to access the supernatural peace of God, you must learn to distinguish between the natural report of the world, and the report of heaven and the Word of God.

When trouble comes, we ask the Lord what He has to say about it.

When a hopeless report is given to us, we ask, "What is the report of the Lord?"

- Numbers 13: Consider the 12 spies; 10 gave a natural report that the KJV Bible calls an evil report, and 2 gave a report of faith and victory. Joshua and Caleb factored in the promises of God and saw the Giants in the land as easy prey for God's people to overcome.
- II Kings 6:8-23: Elisha and his servant are facing a contingent of enemy soldiers sent to arrest and kill them. Elisha sees beyond the natural to the spiritual realm and tells his servant that the angel armies around them outnumber the meager force sent to arrest them.

It is so important that we become a people of faith and vision. That we grab ahold of what God is saying in every circumstance. Your peace depends of knowing the report of the Lord. *"Do not be afraid; only believe."*

*[20]Now to Him who is able to do **exceedingly abundantly above** all that we ask or think, according to the power that works in us, [21]to Him be glory in the church by Christ Jesus to all generations, forever and ever. Amen.*
~ Ephesians 3:20-21

The mindset of peace is a mindset of faith and trust. To have hope is to have peace; you must believe in a God of hope who answers prayers. You must believe in a God of miracles, not just that God is capable of miraculous intervention, but that

He wills to do so. Listen to those three words in Ephesians 3:20: <u>Exceedingly</u>, <u>abundantly</u> and <u>above</u>. That is not the language of small-mindedness or of weak faith; those are the words of super-abundance. Every good gift flows down from a generous heavenly Father.

> *For God has not given us a spirit of fear,*
> *but of power and of love and of a sound mind.*
> *~ II Timothy 1:7*

This verse tells us that God has given us the power to renounce overwhelming fear. We can reach for the grace to receive His abundant peace. Being at peace doesn't mean that we ignore reality, or deny the situation. It just means that we trust God despite the evil report. Jesus pulls us above the stress of the moment into a higher faith. *"Do not be afraid, only believe."*

Prayer:
Dear heavenly Father,
Help me to hear Your report of hope and faith. I refuse to stay in a state of panic, anxiety, or fear; I choose to trust and obey. Show me the promises that I should listen to and look at as I face life's challenges.
I receive Your peace now, in Jesus' name, Amen.

Day 9

Do Not Strive

⁷So He told a parable to those who were invited, when He noted how they chose the best places, saying to them: ⁸"When you are invited by anyone to a wedding feast, do not sit down in the best place, lest one more honorable than you be invited by him; ⁹and he who invited you and him come and say to you, 'Give place to this man,' and then you begin with shame to take the lowest place. ¹⁰But when you are invited, go and sit down in the lowest place, so that when he who invited you comes he may say to you, 'Friend, go up higher.' Then you will have glory in the presence of those who sit at the table with you. ¹¹For whoever exalts himself will be humbled, and he who humbles himself will be exalted."
~ Luke 14:7-11

There is nothing wrong with some healthy ambition and a drive to succeed. But when it causes you to lose your peace, then it's not worth it. Let me give you an example: I was newly married and I believed it was time I started an independent church. I didn't think any of the Pastors in the area knew what they were doing. So, I started filling out the required documents for a non-profit organization status. I no sooner put my pen to the paper when God spoke to my spirit, *"What are you doing?"* That was it. Just one question. In that one question, I knew I was acting in pride and striving ahead of God. That night my wife, Nicole, had a dream that she had given birth to a deformed baby. The Lord spoke to her in the dream and said, *"That is what your church is going to look like. Your disciples will be deformed and imbalanced. You're not ready to pastor your own church yet."* I didn't need any prophetic words after that. We submitted to a local church and found peace again.

You are not going to access God's Supernatural peace if you are striving outside of God's will. We must submit our plans and purposes to God. We must wait for the Lord to say, "Come up higher." Also, it does no good to compete and compare with those around you. You are your own person. For every person God calls, there is a unique process. Your process is not going to look like anyone else's. There may be similarities, but you will have your own timeframe as well.

> *In all your ways acknowledge Him,*
> *And He shall direct your paths.*
> *~ Proverbs 3:6*

Notice it says, "In ALL your ways acknowledge Him." It's dangerous business to make major decisions outside of God's consultation. I'm reminded of a story in the Bible where King Saul was waiting for Samuel the prophet to make a sacrifice just before the army engaged an innumerable host of Philistines in battle. The longer Samuel delayed his arrival to make the sacrifice, the more fear spread through Saul's army. The fear and impending doom reached a tipping point where men were starting to desert. In a state of exasperation, Saul did what was unlawful; he made the sacrifice without the prophet Samuel. Amazingly, as soon as Saul had completed the unlawful sacrifice, Samuel showed up and rebuked him (see I Samuel 13:1-15). Listen to King Saul's excuse:

> [11]*And Samuel said, "What have you done?" Saul said,*
> *"When I saw that the people were scattered from me, and that*
> *you did not come within the days appointed,*
> *and that the Philistines gathered together at Michmash,*
> [12]*then I said, 'The Philistines will now come down on me at*

> *Gilgal, and I have not made supplication to the Lord.'*
> **Therefore I felt compelled**, *and offered a burnt offering."*
> ~ I Samuel 13:11-12

Note the phrase that I emphasized, "*Therefore I felt compelled.*" The Holy Spirit will *lead* you, but the devil and your flesh will *push* you and compel you. If you are being tempted to do something against the Word, then you know you're being pushed outside of God's peace. Self-will and striving are the number one enemy of the Christian. And here you thought it was the Devil, Satan, that ol' slew foot. Nope, look in the mirror. When you don't have peace, search your heart and ask yourself if you are striving? If King Saul would have just waited a little longer, God would have done a miracle and Saul would have ended up in the Hall of Faith.

> *Do not be like the horse or like the mule, which have no*
> *understanding, which must be harnessed with bit and bridle,*
> *Else they will not come near you.*
> ~ Psalm 32:9

The horse tends to run ahead and the mule tends to lag behind. You don't have to be either, you can be right on time with God; moving with the rhythm of the Holy Spirit. You can know the times and the seasons.

Prayer:
Dear Heavenly Father,
Nothing is worth sacrificing my peace. I need Your
peace to live victoriously and enjoy Your blessings.
I repent for striving ahead of You, and I repent for
lagging behind. Help me to be right on time. Help me to
be sensitive to Your leading.
In Jesus' name, Amen

Day 10

Praying Through to Peace 1

⁶Be anxious for nothing, but in everything by prayer and supplication, with thanksgiving, let your requests be made known to God; ⁷and the peace of God, which surpasses all understanding, will guard your hearts and minds through Christ Jesus.
~ Philippians 4:6-7

How is your anxiety level? The amount of anxiety you have is in direct proportion to your prayer life. Let me restate that; the cure for an anxious heart is praying through to peace. When I speak about praying through to peace, I'm not talking about a quick little "Please bless the food, Oh Lord," type of prayer. I am talking about praying in tongues and in your vernacular language until you get a peace that surpasses understanding.

Before we proceed, I'm assuming that you have been Baptized in the Holy Spirit with the physical evidence of praying in tongues. If you do not have a prayer language, find a Spirit-filled church, and ask them to pray and lay hands on you to receive the Baptism in the Holy Spirit. I can't tell you how crucial this is for you to access God's supernatural peace. You need the power of the Holy Spirit to go to the next level of victorious living.

1. There is a difference between baptism in water and baptism in the Holy Spirit.

For John truly baptized with water, but you shall be baptized with the Holy Spirit not many days from now. ~ *Acts 1:5*

Jesus distinguished the difference between being baptized with water and being baptized with the Holy Spirit. The Greek word for "baptized" is baptizo (Strong's #908). It means to dip or immerse. When we are baptized in water, we identify with the death, burial, and resurrection of Christ. We are accepting an invitation to be a part of the Christian community. When we are baptized in the Holy Spirit, we are immersed in the power of God to live victoriously.

2. There is a difference between being indwelt with the Holy Spirit at conversion (Born Again), and baptism in the Holy Spirit.

But you are not in the flesh but in the Spirit, if indeed the Spirit of God dwells in you. Now if anyone does not have the Spirit of Christ, he is not His. ~ *Romans 8:9*

The Spirit of Christ is another name for the Holy Spirit. When you repent for your sins and make Jesus your Lord and Savior, you are indwelt with the Holy Spirit.

Not by works of righteousness which we have done, but according to His mercy He saved us, through the washing of regeneration and renewing of the Holy Spirit. ~ *Titus 3:5*

What a glorious thing to be indwelt with the Holy Spirit. We become born again into a new life with Christ. Being indwelt by the Spirit will get you into fellowship with God, and it will get you into heaven, but it's not enough to access a super victorious life. Jesus made it imperative to be baptized in the Holy Spirit (see Acts 1:4-8).

After Philip converted the whole city of Samaria to the Lord, the apostles sent Peter and John to lay hands on them to be baptized in the Holy Spirit (see Acts 8:14-23). Being baptized in the Holy Spirit was not an alternative, it was an imperative. If being Born Again and baptized in water was enough, why send Peter and John to Samaria to lay hands on them and pray for them to be overflowing with the Spirit?

3. You need to be baptized in the Holy Spirit so that you can pray in tongues.

> *And they were all filled with the Holy Spirit and began to **speak with other tongues**, as the Spirit gave them utterance.* ~ *Acts 2:4*

Being able to pray in tongues is crucial to you accessing and maintaining God's supernatural peace in your life. Praying in tongues will build you up in the inner man (see Jude 20, I Corinthians 14:4). Praying in tongues is praying divine secrets directly to God; you are praying the perfect will of God.

> *For he who speaks in a tongue does not speak*
> *to men but to God, for no one understands him;*
> *however, in the spirit he speaks mysteries.*
> *~ I Corinthians 14:2*

> *Now He who searches the hearts knows what the*
> *mind of the Spirit is, because He makes intercession*
> *for the saints according to the will of God.*
> *~ Romans 8:27*

In the next Devotional, I will talk further about praying through to peace. Being baptized in the Holy Spirit, and receiving a personal prayer language is paramount for walking in God's peace. If you have been baptized in the Holy Spirit and have not used your prayer language, or you desire to pray in tongues now, then say this prayer out loud with me:

Dear Lord Jesus,
I want to be baptized in the Holy Spirit. John the Baptist said that You are the one who baptizes with the Holy Spirit.

["I indeed baptize you with water unto repentance,
but He who is coming after me is mightier than I,
whose sandals I am not worthy to carry.
He will baptize you with the Holy Spirit and fire."
~ Matthew 3:11]

Baptize me now Lord Jesus. I want to obey Your
command in Acts 1 to get baptized in the Holy Spirit. By
faith, I lift my hands and receive Your free gift. I will now
speak with tongues. Thank You, for the Holy Spirit and
His power in my life.
In Jesus' name, Amen

Begin now to speak in tongues by faith. Words are just syllables; speak forth the words that come to you. "*Therefore I say to you, whatever things you ask when you pray, believe that you receive them, and you will have them.*" Mark 11:24.

44While Peter was still speaking these words, the Holy Spirit
fell upon all those who heard the word. 45And those of the
circumcision who believed were astonished, as many as
came with Peter, because the gift of the Holy Spirit
had been poured out on the Gentiles also.
46For they heard them speak with tongues and magnify God.
~ Acts 10:44-46

Day 11

Praying Through to Peace 11

*⁶Be anxious for nothing, but in everything by prayer and
supplication, with thanksgiving, let your requests
be made known to God; ⁷and the peace of God,
which surpasses all understanding, will guard
your hearts and minds through Christ Jesus.
~ Philippians 4:6-7*

*(Anxiety: A feeling of worry, nervousness, or unease,
typically about an imminent event or something with an
uncertain outcome.)*

Many times, anxiety is a spiritual feeling; the Holy Spirit may be pulling you into intercession. When I feel a lot of anxiety, I go into prayer mode. I pray in tongues until I get peace. Praying though to the peace of God has become a lost art. Old school Pentecostals know what it means to pray though to the peace of God. When you have prayed until you are at total peace, you will be forever changed. You will never settle for genuflect prayers again. What is having peace in your mind and spirit worth to you? You can give God just a tip, or you can give a sacrifice. You can be spiritually lazy, or you can exercise your spirit by praying in tongues. You can be a victim to your circumstances, or you can be a victorious overcomer. When the Bible says to *"Be anxious for nothing,"* it means that you never have to let anxiety rule your life. You have been given the power to pray through to peace.

But you, beloved, build yourselves up [founded] on your most
holy faith [make progress, rise like an edifice higher and
higher], praying in the Holy Spirit.
~ Jude 1:20 AMPC

When the Bible tells you that by praying in the Holy Spirit you will build up your most holy faith, it means it. Praying in the Spirit is praying under the unction of the Spirit. It usually takes me 10 to 20 minutes to pray through to some peace. I dare you to try it. Lift up your hands and start telling God how awesome He is, and then start thanking Him. Pray in tongues for 20 minutes nonstop, and then see how you feel. Your faith will be built up and you will be more at peace. What have you got to lose? It's obvious that all the entertainment, distractions, and medications don't get the job done.

What is the conclusion then? **I will pray with the spirit,** *and I*
will also pray with the understanding. I will sing with the spirit,
and I will also sing with the understanding.
~ I Corinthians 14:15

Notice how praying with understanding is the juxtaposition of praying in the spirit. This means that praying in the spirit is praying in tongues. Also notice that praying in the spirit is an act of the will; you can do it any time you will it so. Paul said "*I* **will** *pray in the spirit.*" You don't have to wait for some spiritual feeling to come over you, provoking you to pray in tongues. When you are baptized in the Holy Spirit with the outward physical evidence of speaking in tongues, you can pray in tongues any time you desire from that point on.

One of the greatest examples in the Bible of someone praying through to peace is Hannah (see I Samuel, chapter 1). She hadn't been able to have children and, in her heart, she knew this was wrong. She pressed in to God with fasting. At the door of the Tabernacle she prayed and wept in anguish. At first, the High Priest Eli thought she was drunk, but when he found out it was a woman praying in sincerity of heart, he blessed her and pronounced, in a prophetic way, that her request was granted by God.

> ¹³*Now Hannah spoke in her heart; only her lips moved, but her voice was not heard. Therefore Eli thought she was drunk.* ¹⁴*So Eli said to her, "How long will you be drunk? Put your wine away from you!"* ¹⁵*But Hannah answered and said, "No, my lord, I am a woman of sorrowful spirit. I have drunk neither wine nor intoxicating drink, but have poured out my soul before the Lord,* ¹⁶*"Do not consider your maidservant a wicked woman, for out of the abundance of my complaint and grief I have spoken until now."* ¹⁷**Then Eli answered and said, "Go in peace, and the God of Israel grant your petition which you have asked of Him."** ¹⁸*And she said, "Let your maidservant find favor in your sight." So the woman went her way and ate, and her face was no longer sad.*
> ~ *I Samuel 1:13-18*

Notice that after Eli pronounced God's blessing on Hannah, *she found peace.* She prayed through until she knew in her spirit that everything was going to be all right. She knew by faith that her petition was granted. Nine months later, she gave birth to the prophet Samuel. Look how her prayer victory helped a whole nation. *You* are so needed; your prayer victories will be written in heaven's book of prayer heroes. Many lives will be influenced for good because of *your* prayer victories.

Challenge:
Pray in tongues for 20 minutes nonstop. If you still don't have peace, pray in tongues for another 20 minutes. Repeat until the peace of God that passes understanding guards your heart (emotions) and mind (thoughts).

If you have not yet received a prayer language, refer back to Day 10 and recite that prayer again.

Day 12

The Keeping Power of God

*²³Now may **the God of peace** Himself **sanctify you completely;**
and may your whole spirit, soul, and body be preserved
blameless at the coming of our Lord Jesus Christ.
²⁴He who calls you is faithful, **who also will do it.**
~ I Thessalonians 5:23-24*

Having faith in God's keeping power over your life will bring you tremendous peace. Once you are His, He watches over you, protects you, cherishes you, and sanctifies you. The process of sanctification is when God does a maturing and purifying work in your life as you follow Him. There is a constant setting apart for His holy purposes. You are no longer for the world and common things; you are a king and priest to the Most High God (see Revelation 1:6).

*⁹But you are a **chosen generation, a royal priesthood,
a holy nation**, His own **special people**, that you may
proclaim the praises of Him who called you out
of darkness into His marvelous light; ¹⁰who once
were not a people but **are now the people of God**,
who had not obtained mercy but now have obtained mercy.
~ I Peter 2:9-10*

YOU ARE GOD'S SPECIAL TREASURE

There is a great Bible illustration about how special you and I are, and what it means to be set apart for great and holy purposes (please read Daniel 5).

When the Tabernacle and Temple were completed, every vessel, table, and altar was anointed with the Holy Oil (see Leviticus 8:10). Moses also sprinkled blood on every vessel used by the priests to worship Yahweh (see Hebrews 9:21). A King of Babylon used some of the golden cups taken from the Jerusalem Temple for a drunken party (see Daniel 5:3). That evening, during the vile celebration, a hand appeared and wrote a judgment on the wall. That very evening, the King who had used vessels sanctified for holy purposes in his drunken orgy, was deposed and killed (see Daniel 5:30-31).

You have been anointed by the Holy Spirit and the blood of Christ has been sprinkled on your heart and life. You are God's special treasure. He will judge any attempt by man or devil to use you for an inglorious purpose.

> *For you are a holy people to the Lord your God; the Lord*
> *your God has chosen you to be a people for Himself, a special*
> *treasure above all the peoples on the face of the earth.*
> *~ Deuteronomy 7:6*

YOU ARE BEING CHANGED AND MATURED

God's keeping power also means that He is growing you by the work of the Holy Spirit. You are going from faith to faith (see Romans 1:16-17), strength to strength (see Psalm 84:7), glory to glory (see II Corinthians 3:18). The sanctifying work of the Holy Spirit is both **positional** and a **process**. When you made Jesus the Lord of your life, you were made right with God. You were washed and regenerated by the Holy Spirit. When you are **positionally** right with God, you can go directly to heaven when you die.

> *For He made Him who knew no sin to be sin for us, that we*
> *might become the righteousness of God in Him.*
> *~ II Corinthians 5:21*

*Not by works of righteousness which we have done,
but according to His mercy He saved us, through the washing
of regeneration and renewing of the Holy Spirit.*
~ Titus 3:5

Sanctification is also a process. The keeping power of God is changing you and adapting you for greater victory and to overcome anything the world can throw at you. God is working in you and empowering you to overcome.

*I can do all things [which He has called me to do] through Him
who strengthens and empowers me [to fulfill His purpose—I
am self-sufficient in Christ's sufficiency; I am ready for
anything and equal to anything through Him who infuses
me with inner strength and confident peace.]*
~ Philippians 4:13 AMP

*And we all, with unveiled face, continually seeing as in a mirror
the glory of the Lord, are progressively being transformed
into His image from [one degree of] glory to [even more]
glory, which comes from the Lord, [who is] the Spirit.*
~ II Corinthians 3:18 AMP

PROMISES OF GOD'S KEEPING POWER

*Now to Him who is **able** to keep you from stumbling,
and to present you faultless Before the presence of
His glory with exceeding joy.*
~ Jude 1:24

*Being confident of this very thing, that He who has begun a
good work in you will complete it until the day of Jesus Christ.*
~ Philippians 1:6

*27"My sheep hear My voice, and I know them, and they follow
Me. 28And I give them eternal life, and they shall never perish;
neither shall anyone snatch them out of My hand.
29My Father, who has given them to Me, is greater than all;
and no one is able to snatch them out of My Father's hand.
30I and My Father are one."*
~ John 10:27-30

> *Who shall separate us from the love of Christ? Shall*
> *tribulation, or distress, or persecution, or famine, or nakedness,*
> *or peril, or sword?*
> *~ Romans 8:35*

These scriptures should give you great peace knowing that God is your keeper and preserver. I believe that a person can forfeit their salvation, but my question is, why would anyone want to? It's hard to walk away from God. It's possible, but difficult to do. He will send angels and prophets to speak to your heart, and He will put up roadblocks to protect you. He will discipline His wayward children. His keeping power is mighty. His grace is far-reaching. His power is unshakable.

Your assignment is to read Psalm 121 twice, personalizing it as you read. Then let God's protective peace assure you of His faithfulness.

~ Psalm 121 KJV (personalized):

> *¹I will lift up my eyes to the hills—*
> *From whence comes my help?*
> *²My help comes from the LORD,*
> *Who made heaven and earth.*
> *³He will not allow my foot to be moved;*
> *He who keeps me will not slumber.*
> *⁴Behold, He who keeps Israel*
> *Shall neither slumber nor sleep.*
> *⁵The LORD is my keeper;*
> *The LORD is my shade at my right hand.*
> *⁶The sun shall not strike me by day,*
> *Nor the moon by night.*
> *⁷The LORD shall preserve me from all evil;*
> *He shall preserve my soul.*
> *⁸The LORD shall preserve my going out and my coming in*
> *From this time forth, and even forevermore.*

Day 13

Peace in the Time of Famine

*[18]The Lord knows the days of the upright, and their inheritance shall be forever. [19]They shall not be ashamed in the evil time, and **in the days of famine they shall be satisfied.***
~ Psalm 37:18-19

*[19]He shall deliver you in six troubles, Yes, in seven no evil shall touch you. [20]**In famine He shall redeem you from death**, and in war from the power of the sword. [21]You shall be hidden from the scourge of the tongue, and you shall not be afraid of destruction when it comes. [22]**You shall laugh at destruction and famine**, and you shall not be afraid of the beasts of the earth.*
~ Job 5:19-22

In times of uncertainty, we can get pretty stressed. God has given us promises to claim regarding His provisions in times of famine. No matter what the economy is going through, and no matter where you live in the world, His promises are *yes* and *amen*. The promises of God are sure and steadfast.

One Sunday, during the 2020 Covid-19 pandemic, I quoted Psalm 37:19 to the church: *"You shall not be ashamed in evil times and in the days of famine you shall be satisfied."* And then I said, "I want you to know that this promise is always good, unless you are in a famine, then it doesn't work."

You should have seen how the congregation responded. The looks on their faces said, "What? Has Pastor lost it? Has too much education caused him to not believe God's promises?"

I let my statement hang out there for a few seconds and then added, "Of course God's promises will work for us in famine! They are true *especially* in famine." I then continued with "How about this verse? *²I will say of the Lord, He is my refuge and my fortress; My God, in Him I will trust. ³Surely He shall deliver you from the snare of the fowler and from the perilous pestilence. Psalm 91:2-3.* I want you to know that this promise from Psalm 91 is only good when there is NO pestilence or pandemic in the land."

The point I made was clear; we can't let fear and evil reports nullify the promises of God. When there is famine or pestilence, we still have the promises of God to meditate on. Walk in wisdom and take precautions, but then trust God to take care of you. Faith and trust are the bridge to supernatural peace every time. No matter what, we trust the Lord and look to His unchangeable promises.

- Isaac sowed in the land during a famine and reaped 100-fold (see Genesis 26:1-14).
- Jacob and his family went to Egypt during a famine, and Joseph situated them in the best of the land; the land of Goshen. There, they prospered in the time of famine (see Genesis 47:27).
- Elijah prayed that it would not rain for 3½ years, and then, during that time of famine, God sent ravens and a widow to feed him (see I Kings 17:1-16).
- When there was nothing to eat, Jesus multiplied bread and fish to feed 5,000 people (see Mark 6:30-42).

The Bible is replete with example after example of supernatural supply to those who trust in God. Be at peace.

If you are doing all you know to do, trust and be at peace. Here are some promises of supernatural supply:

God has an unlimited supply

And my God shall supply all your need according to His riches in glory by Christ Jesus. ~ *Philippians 4:19*

God supplies for those who seek Him

Oh, fear the Lord, you His saints! There is no want to those who fear Him. The young lions lack and suffer hunger; But those who seek the Lord shall not lack any good thing. ~ *Psalm 34:9-10*

God supplies for those who walk uprightly

For the Lord God is a sun and shield; The Lord will give grace and glory; No good thing will He withhold from those who walk uprightly. ~ *Psalm 84:11*

God supplies for those who tithe and give offerings

"Bring all the tithes into the storehouse, that there may be food in My house, and try Me now in this," Says the Lord of hosts, "If I will not open for you the windows of heaven and pour out for you such blessing that there will not be room enough to receive it." ~ *Malachi 3:10*

Now may He who supplies seed to the sower, and bread for food, supply and multiply the seed you have sown and increase the fruits of your righteousness. ~ *II Corinthians 9:10*

God supplies for those who work

Let him who stole steal no longer, but rather let him labor, working with his hands what is good, that he may have something to give him who has need. ~ *Ephesians 4:28*

[11]*That you also aspire to lead a quiet life, to mind your own business, and to work with your own hands, as we commanded you,* [12]*that you may walk properly toward those who are outside, and that you may lack nothing.*
~ *I Thessalonians 4:11-12*

God supplies by His great grace

And God is able to make all grace abound toward you, that you, always having all sufficiency in all things, may have an abundance for every good work.
~ *II Corinthians 9:8*

Plan of action:
Quote all these verses about God's provisions aloud
until worry about lack leaves you. Receive God's peace.
Release your faith and God's blessings by giving tithes
and offerings unto the Lord.

Day 14

The God of Hope

Now may the God of hope fill you with all joy and peace
in believing, that you may abound in hope
by the power of the Holy Spirit.
~ Romans 15:13

Our God is not only the God of peace, but He is the God of Hope as well. Hope is having a positive outlook for the future. The amount of joy and peace that you and I experience is directly connected to how much hope we have. Hopefulness emanates from the Holy Spirit. He is the Spirit of truth, and truth brings hope. If we are hopeless, it means that we are believing a lie from the enemy. The God of the Bible will *never* tell you hopeless lies. A situation may seem hopeless, but there is still hope to be found. Even when we face death, there is hope for the Christian.

I am the God of Abraham, the God of Isaac, and the God of
Jacob? God is not the God of the dead, but of the living.
~ Matthew 22:32

When I was in my early 20s, I traveled with a Christian rock band. We played and shared our testimonies at coffee houses, churches, and Jesus festivals (pretty much anywhere people would listen to us). We wanted to please God and debated whether it was right for us to sign our autographs after performances. We didn't want to bring glory to ourselves, but only to God. And yet, we didn't want to reject anyone who asked us to sign a poster, album, or t-shirt. I finally resolved that I would only sign an autograph along with a scripture verse reference. I figured that if I left someone with just me, it would not help them much, but if I left them with more of God and His Word, I would be helping them for life. My favorite verse to reference is in the book of Jeremiah:

> *11For I know the thoughts that I think toward you, says the Lord, **thoughts of peace and not of evil, to give you a future and a hope.** 12Then you will call upon Me and go and pray to Me, and I will listen to you. 13And you will seek Me and find Me, when you search for Me with all your heart.*
> *~ Jeremiah 29:11-13*

God thinks good thoughts toward you, thoughts that give you peace and hope. Begin to believe again. Begin to hope again. Reject hopeless lies. When you start to believe, then the power of the Holy Spirit kicks in, (*...believing, that you may abound in hope by the power of the Holy Spirit. Romans 15:13*). When we draw near to God, then He draws near to us (see James 4:8). We will find Him when we seek Him with all our heart.

Prayer:
Dear God,
I receive Your hope, joy, and peace. I reject lying thoughts that attempt to steal my peace and hope. Direct me to Bible verses that speak to my situation. I will draw nigh to You, God. I will seek You and You will be found. I choose to believe the truth that brings hope to my soul. I rest in Your peace, oh God. I love you.
In Jesus' name, Amen

Being at Peace with Yourself and Others

If it is possible,
as much as depends on you,
live peaceably with all men.
~ Romans 12:18

Day 15

Forgive to Keep Your Peace

²⁵And whenever you stand praying, if you have anything against anyone, forgive him, that your Father in heaven may also forgive you your trespasses. ²⁶But if you do not forgive, neither will your Father in heaven forgive your trespasses.
~ Mark 11:25-26

Looking carefully lest anyone fall short of the grace of God; lest any root of bitterness springing up cause trouble, and by this many become defiled.
~ Hebrews 12:15

It stands to reason that unforgiveness will rob us of supernatural peace. It's easy to tell someone *else* that they need to forgive. It's easy to point out someone *else* who is bitter. Let's face it, some things are really hard to forgive. There are levels of offense, and some things are easier to forgive than others. Nevertheless, we are to reach for God's grace in every situation and forgive by faith. I've heard it said that unforgiveness is like drinking poison hoping the other person dies.

It's important to note that there is a difference between forgiveness and trust. I can forgive someone who abuses me, but unless that person repents and acknowledges the abuse, I'm no longer going to associate with them. Why would I subject myself to continued abuse? Once trust is lost, in many cases it takes time to rebuild. Forgiveness is not always a reconciliation of the relationship. In some cases, the person you need to forgive is already in the grave.

Let me tell you of a man's story of forgiveness and freedom. During my first years of Bible College, I was a sales manager for an office equipment company and delivered products to a lawyer's office. As I conversed with the lawyer, he discovered that I was a ministry student. He told me his story and gave me permission to share it. He told me that God had sent me to him so that I could share his story and help others. Since then, whenever I speak on forgiveness, I honor his request to share his story.

That man grew up hating his father, an alcoholic who embarrassed him. Every boy wants to look up to their dad, but his dad was the town drunk. He swore that he would never be like him, but when he was in college he started drinking and partying with friends. He quickly descended into alcoholism. He had become what he hated. The family curse had found him. He hated his father, and now he hated himself too.

One night in a drunken stupor, he decided to kill himself. There was a cold rain that night as he drove out to the bridge from which he planned to jump. As he stood out on the edge of the bridge, he looked down into the murky, churning water far below. He then looked up as the icy rain pelted his face. At that point, he had a vision: he saw Jesus on the cross, and heard Jesus say, "Father, forgive them for they know not what they do." It suddenly occurred to the man that he was to forgive his father. He began to wail and weep as he repeated Jesus' words from the cross, "Father, I forgive my father, for he was caught up in the same curse that I'm caught in. He didn't know what he was doing." Immediately he felt the curse of alcoholism break and a huge weight lift. He was instantly stone-sober. He gave his life to Christ right there and never touched another drop of alcohol from that day forward. Forgiveness had delivered him and saved him that cold wet night.

There is another lesson here; if we do not forgive, we risk becoming what we hate. In this lawyer's case, he became an alcoholic like his Dad. Don't become what you won't forgive. We must forgive even when we don't *feel* like doing so. Forgiveness is an act of faith, and feelings will eventually follow faith.

Who do you have to forgive? Say this prayer with me.

Dear Heavenly Father,
By faith I forgive _____ (say their name/
names).

Day 16

Forgive by Faith

¹⁴For if you forgive men their trespasses, your heavenly Father will also forgive you. ¹⁵But if you do not forgive men their trespasses, neither will your Father forgive your trespasses.
~ Matthew 6:14-15

God would not ask us to do anything that wasn't possible with faith and His grace.

A Pastor friend of mine pioneered and pastored his church. He was pastoring for three years before marrying a very sweet young woman whom he met at a dynamic college campus church. After they were married, for some strange demonic reason, the women in the church started attacking this Pastor's wife very brutally. The Pastor warned and admonished the attackers, but it didn't stop the mean-girl type of bullying. One day the Pastor just closed the church down. I mean, he shut it down and stopped pastoring. He loved his wife more than the church he had pioneered.

Can you imagine what this young pastor's wife went through? Most women want to support their husbands and help them to be successful, but now she felt as though she contributed to his failure. In her mind, she was the cause of the church closing down. She fought with feelings of hatred toward those women who had bullied, rejected, and slandered her. She didn't think she was capable of forgiving them. She not only hated those women, but she hated herself for having such bitter feelings.

Day after day, and week after week, she prayed for them and forgave them, **by faith**, for two years. As much as she forgave them by faith, she still felt anger in her heart. Then one day she was in the grocery store and encountered one of the ladies who had been so resentful toward her. She was amazed that there were no feelings of hatred and anger toward her as they talked. In fact, just the opposite; she felt a supernatural love for this woman and a genuine concern for her wellbeing. As she reflected on this divine appointment in meeting up with a former tormentor, she thanked God that her feelings caught up with her confession of faith. It took two years, but she forgave out of obedience to God and her faith was rewarded. She was set free from the seething anger and bitter hatred. What's more, she genuinely wanted those ladies who attacked her to be blessed. I don't know if they will end up being best friends, but this was a huge breakthrough.

I've heard it said that faith is the engine of the train and feelings are the caboose. Eventually our feelings will follow our confession of faith. We walk by faith and not by sight. We are obedient by faith until feelings come into alignment with the Word of God. For this amazing pastor's wife, it took two years until her feelings caught up with her confession of faith and forgiveness. Continue to forgive by faith until the anger and hatred lift.

Every once in a while I think about a situation where someone has wronged me or wounded me and I'll start getting angry about it all over again. When this happens, I remind myself of the testimony of this pastor's wife. I want to be like her and tenaciously forgive until all tormenting feelings of anger and bitterness are gone.

Say this prayer with me and forgive by faith until your feelings line up with your confession of faith. Remember, forgiveness doesn't always mean that the relationship will be restored, but it's a start. The Holy Spirit will give you peace and speak to you about whether you should attempt to restore a relationship or not.

Thank You, Father, for forgiving me and accepting me into the family of God. I now forgive by faith. I refuse to live in bitterness and hatred. This life is a gift from God and I choose to live it to the fullest. I vow to continue to forgive by faith until my feelings align themselves to my confession of faith.
In Jesus' name, Amen

Day 17

Live Peaceably with All Men

If it is possible, as much as depends on you,
live peaceably with all men.
~ Romans 12:18

We are to exhaust all avenues to peace. As much as depends on us we must do our part.

As a Pastor, I have counseled people who were determined to divorce their spouse. I can never tell someone what to do, I am just an advisor, and I bring the Word of God to bear on their issues. I almost always advise the person considering divorce to make sure their conscience is clear before God. They must be brutally honest with themselves and ask the question: Have I done everything possible to make this marriage work? *"If it is possible, as much as depends on you, live peaceably with all men."*

Many times, after challenging a person considering divorce with that question, they discover an avenue of peace. It's not always the quick and easy solution, but whoever said doing the right thing is always easy. Because marital situations can be so varied and complicated, it's good to seek wise counsel.

⁵Woe is me, that I dwell in Meshech, That I dwell among the tents of Kedar! ⁶My soul has dwelt too long with

> *one who hates peace. ⁷**I am for peace; But***
> ***when I speak, they are for war.***
> *~ Psalm 120:5-7*

But what if *you* are for peace but *they* are for war? Sometimes it's impossible to be at peace with someone, or a particular group of people. That's why the scripture says, "*If it be possible*" and, "*as much as depends on you.*" If you've done everything you can to bring peace, and they are still for war, then you must walk away.

Who are the people dwelling in Meshech and the tents of Kedar? Meshech was a brutal northern tribe, and Kedar represented nomadic people that were always at war. Their hand was against every man, and every man's hand was against them. Apparently there are super contentious people in this world who are always stirring up drama. Don't receive a guilt trip for not achieving peace with people who always want war.

If war is unavoidable, your first action is to wage war in the Heavenlies with prayer. Pray for your enemies. Pray for God's strategy in the conflict. His strategy may be to confront them, it may be to bless them, or it may simply be to avoid them. Don't act rashly without consulting your Heavenly Father.

> *Now thanks be to God who **always leads us in triumph** in*
> *Christ, and through us diffuses the fragrance of*
> *His knowledge in every place.*
> *~ II Corinthians 2:14*

Our God promises us that He will always lead us to victory. Even when we seem to be losing, there is a victory to be achieved. There is a path to peace. If there must be a war, you can rest in the peaceful assurance that the Lord will lead you through to triumph. There is peace in the promise of victory. There is peace in obedience. There is peace on the other side of war.

One finale encouragement: before going to war make sure you are in the right by doing some real heart-searching. This is why the first thing you must do in a war is pray. Prayer for the Christian is not just a monologue, which is a one-sided talk. Prayer is a dialogue whereby we talk to God and listen to His response. He will speak to you. He will bear witness to your heart as to what it is that you should do. This will require waiting on Him and some deep heart-searching. When Abraham Lincoln was asked by a reporter if he believed God was on his side, this was his response: "Sir, my concern is not whether God is on our side; my greatest concern is to be on God's side, for God is always right."

Pray this with me:

Dear God,
Help me to do everything I can to be at peace with
people. Give me wisdom and surround me with wise
counselors. Let me hear what the Holy Spirit is saying to
me. Give me Your strategy for victory. I don't want to be
at war with anyone. I know You will show me the path
to peace without surrendering my dignity. I am willing
to humble myself, but I know You don't wish for me to
compromise to sin.
In the name of Jesus, I pray, Amen

Thus says the Lord, your Redeemer, The Holy One of Israel: "I
*am the Lord your God, Who teaches you to profit, **Who leads***
you by the way you should go."
~ Isaiah 48:17

To give light to those who sit in darkness and the shadow of
*death, **to guide our feet into the way of peace.***
~ Luke 1:79

Day 18

Peace Through Obedience

*¹My son, do not forget my law, but let your heart keep
my commands; ²For length of days and long life
and peace they will add to you.*
~ Proverbs 3:1-2

You can lose your peace when you are disobedient and out
of the will of God. Some people are rebellious and wonder why
they are being tormented by demons. The supernatural peace
of God comes through obedience to the will of God. His Word is
His will.

*By pride comes nothing but strife, but with
the well-advised is wisdom.*
~ Proverbs 13:10

Pride and refusing to admit that you are wrong is the basis
for strife, division, and unrest. When there is no peace, someone
is in pride and rebellion.

- Pride and rebellion in the workplace causes strife
- Pride and rebellion in the home causes strife
- Pride and rebellion in our country causes strife

*For where envy and self-seeking exist,
confusion and every evil thing are there.*
~ James 3:16

Notice that confusion is the fruit of envy and self-seeking. God does not want you in confusion. He is not the author of confusion, but of peace (see I Corinthians 14:13).

There is a connection in the Bible between disobedience to God and mental illness. Track with me and let me make my case. I am NOT saying that all mental illness is caused by disobedience (i.e., Depression, Schizophrenia, etc.). But disobedience to God is clearly a main cause for madness, confusion, and paranoia. In Deuteronomy 28, God gives the blessings of obedience and the curses for disobedience. Listen to some of these curses caused by rebellion against God and His Word.

> *The Lord will strike you with **madness** and blindness*
> *and **confusion of heart**.*
> *~ Deuteronomy 28:28*

> *So you shall be driven **mad** because of the sight*
> *which your eyes see.*
> *~ Deuteronomy 28:34*

> *Because, although they knew God, they did not glorify Him as*
> *God, nor were thankful, but became **futile in their thoughts**,*
> *and their foolish hearts were darkened.*
> *~ Romans 1:21*

What I am saying here is that you should live an examined life. Examine your heart today and if there is an area that God wants you to obey, do it. There are sins of commission and sins of omission. If we fail to follow through with something that God wants us to do then we are sinning just as if we had done something evil. I had been feeling a bit down, and I searched my heart regarding these feelings. The Lord convicted me about procrastination in writing this devotional. After I repented for my laziness and distractions, I sat down to write and low and behold, the depressed feelings left me.

Check out this scripture of promised peace:

Peace I leave with you, My peace I give to you; not as the world gives do I give to you. Let not your heart be troubled, neither let it be afraid.
~ John 14:27

As I read the context of this well-known Bible verse promising peace, I discovered that it was sandwiched in by admonishments to obey. There is no peace for the wicked (see Isaiah 48:22).

If you love Me, keep My commandments.
~ John 14:15

Pray this prayer with me:

Dear Father in heaven,
If there is an area in my life that I am being disobedient, please show me. I will submit to God, resist the devil, and he will flee from me. Thank you so much for Your delivering power over my life. As for me and my house, we choose to obey and follow the Lord.
In the mighty name of Jesus, I pray, Amen

23Search me, O God, and know my heart; try me, and know my anxieties; 24and see if there is any wicked way in me, and lead me in the way everlasting.
~ Psalm 139:23-24

Day 19

Peace be Multiplied to You

*²**Grace and peace be multiplied to you in the knowledge of
God and of Jesus our Lord,** ³as His divine power has given to
us all things that pertain to life and godliness, through the
knowledge of Him who called us by glory and virtue,
⁴**by which have been given to us exceedingly great and
precious promises**, that through these you may be
partakers of the divine nature, having escaped
the corruption that is in the world through lust.
~ II Peter 1:2-4*

The knowledge of God brings peace. Wherever the Bible
and the knowledge of God flourishes, there is peace and joy. It's
important that our children are taught the knowledge of God.
Listen to one of God's promises:

*All your children shall be taught by the Lord,
and **great shall be the peace of your children.**
~ Isaiah 54:13*

If the knowledge of God brings peace, then the lack of
knowledge brings destruction:

***My people are destroyed for lack of knowledge.** Because you
have rejected knowledge, I also will reject you from being
priest for Me; because you have forgotten the law
of your God, I also will forget your children.
~ Hosea 4:6*

For the first time in America, we have a generation with many who do not have the knowledge of God. I've spoken with many young people who have only been to church a few times in their life, and some only for weddings and funerals. Most funerals/memorials take place in a funeral home because folks do not attend a church. There are varied reasons why people have not attended or stopped attending church, and as a result, they have not raised their children with the knowledge of God and the Bible. One of my favorite excuses that I've heard over the years is that they don't believe in organized religion. My response has always been, "Well you can come to our church because we're not that organized." And then after a few chuckles, I add, "Do you prefer unorganized religion?" In all fairness, I know what most are trying to say:

1. I don't want anyone telling me what I can and cannot do.

2. There is some sin that I don't want to give up.

3. I don't want to waste my time with something phony. I want something real, raw, and authentic; not something watered down with the traditions of men.

This brings me to another point about the knowledge of God. You can't just give someone facts and information. People need a real encounter with the living God. It's not just knowing about God, it's about knowing Him personally.

*When all that generation had been gathered to their fathers, another generation arose after them who **did not know the Lord nor the work which He had done for Israel.***
~ Judges 2:10

In just one generation, a nation turned from the Lord to idolatry. They did not know God on two levels: they didn't know the works, or deeds of God, and they didn't know God personally. People need to know God in an experiential way; I call it God-encounters. Christianity isn't just a dead religion of philosophical and ethical teachings; it's a relationship with the living God.

> And this is eternal life, **that they may know You,** the only true
> God, and Jesus Christ whom You have sent.
> ~ John 17:3

What makes Christianity unique among other religions of the world is that their other gods are unknowable. The Christian God is a personal God. He wants to have a personal relationship with you. Also, many other religions of the world require you to earn your salvation through a system of works. Only in Christianity is salvation a free gift. *We are not saved* **by** *our works; we are saved* **for** *good works (see Ephesians 2:8-10).* Good works and a changed lifestyle are the outward evidence of a true God-encounter. When you meet God, you are changed. Out of your love for Him, you seek to please Him with your life (see II Corinthians 3:17-18).

To wrap things up, supernatural peace is multiplied to you through the knowledge of God. That knowledge is both biblical information and knowing God personally. There is a difference between knowing about someone and knowing them personally. We must know the author of the Bible and then we can better understand the book. The Holy Spirit is our teacher and applies the scriptures to our lives and situations.

Years ago, I was very discouraged and wanted to quit the ministry. A pastor friend jokingly told me that every Monday he writes a letter of resignation and then tears it up. As I sat in the church sanctuary alone, I began to weep and told the Lord that I was done. Then God brought Psalm 16 to my mind, so I looked it up and this is what I read:

> ^{5}O Lord, You are the portion of my inheritance and my cup;
> You maintain my lot. ^{6}The lines have fallen to me
> in pleasant places; Yes, I have a good inheritance.
> ~ Psalm 16:5-6

The Holy Spirit spoke to my heart and said that God almighty was my inheritance. I have a good inheritance. I quickly repented for wanting to forfeit my inheritance. I will never quit until the Lord tells me to do so. Don't let anyone drive you from the lot God has given to you.

It's important that you commit yourself to a good Bible reading program. The one I recommend is the Discipleship Journal Bible Reading Plan by The Navigators, available on the Navigators' website:

> https://www.navigators.org/wp-content/uploads/
> 2017/04/Discipleship-Journal-Bible-Reading-Plan-
> 9781617479083.pdf

It can also be found on the **You Version Bible** app.

Say this prayer with me:

Dear Father in Heaven,
Help me to understand the Bible. Give me a greater
hunger for You and Your Word. I vow today to be a
disciple and commit myself to the reading and study of
Your Word. I want peace to be multiplied to me through
the knowledge of Jesus. Show me great and mighty
things that I know not.*
In Jesus' name, Amen

*See Jeremiah 33:3

Day 20

Living Free of Offense

Great peace have they which love thy law: and
nothing shall offend them.
~ Psalm 119:165 KJV

There is such a great peace and well-being that comes to the
lovers of your word, and they will never be offended.
~ Psalm 119:165 TPT

There is not much worse than being around petty people. They are often defensive, often in strife with those around them, and often looking for something to be defensive about. It can be a real chore to be around them. Their constant bickering wears on your nerves. You can literally feel the life-force being sucked out of you when you are around them. If you want favor with God and man, do not be a petty person.

Have you ever been to the First Church of the Easily Offended? In a church setting, we don't admit that it's the flesh causing envy, jealousy, and competition. We spiritualize it and say it's a spirit of offense. I'm sure the demonic has something to do with it, but usually after someone invites the devil in. No one wants to come to a church with a bunch of petty, easily offended people. We CAN be bigger people. Check this out: the Bible says that if we are walking in the love of Christ we will not be easily provoked:

> *⁴Love suffers long and is kind; love does not envy; love does not parade itself, is not puffed up; ⁵does not behave rudely, does not seek its own, **is not provoked**, thinks no evil; ⁶does not rejoice in iniquity, but rejoices in the truth; ⁷bears all things, believes all things, hopes all things, endures all things.*
> *~ I Corinthians 13:4-7*

Just to be clear; I'm NOT saying we should submit to bullies and abusers. Suffering legitimate trauma, wounding, and abuse is different from being a whining baby. No matter how tough and loving you are, little offenses may pile up. It takes a lot to get me angry, but everyone has a breaking point. Before we become a raging bear we should lovingly and politely confront offenses.

So, here's my solution to overcoming offense:

1) Don't be a petty person. Let the small insults go.

> *Above all things have intense and unfailing love for one another, for love covers a multitude of sins [forgives and disregards the offenses of others].*
> *~ I Peter 4:8*

2) If someone hurts you, you should confront them. Don't let things build up.

> *Moreover if your brother sins against you, go and tell him his fault between you and him alone. If he hears you, you have gained your brother.*
> *~ Matthew 18:15*

One of the things I love about my wife is that she is not afraid to confront an issue. If she is upset with me, she hunts me down and has it out with me. I always know exactly where she stands. I will never wake up one morning and find a note on the kitchen table that reads, "I've had enough. I have moved to St. Paul. Don't call. We're through." This will never happen. In the first place, she wouldn't say it in a note, where's the fun in that? Secondly, she would force me to confront the issue instead of ignoring it until things are beyond repair. One time we joked about divorce and she said, "I'll never divorce you. Do you think you'll get out of it that easy? No, you're going to have to deal with me."

Years ago I was at a home prayer meeting and the host gave me a prophetic word. It wasn't a "Thus sayeth the Lord" word. It was a Bible verse that he felt led to share with me:

Great peace have they which love thy law:
and nothing shall offend them.
~ Psalm 119:165 KJV

It hit me square between the eyes. I was falling into the petty trap. I was becoming an easily offended person. What's worse, I was the pastor of the church! I got the message from the Lord, "You love my Word. Receive my peace, and don't be easily offended."

Be a lover of the Word of God. It will keep you loving God and loving others. God has given us the grace to rise above offense.

Pray this prayer with me:

Dear Heavenly Father,
Help me to be patient with people. Give me discernment
to know when to confront offense. Reveal to me any
pettiness in my heart. I receive Your grace to be at
peace with others. Thank You for Your Law. I love Your
Word and I receive the great peace that is imparted to
me through it.
In Jesus' name, Amen

Day 21

God Wants to Give You Peace

God wants you to be at peace:

- *Casting all your care upon Him, for He cares for you.*
  ~ I Peter 5:7
- *Peace I leave with you, My peace I give to you; not as the world gives do I give to you. Let not your heart be troubled, neither let it be afraid.*
  ~ John 14:27
- *Now may the Lord of peace Himself give you peace always in every way. The Lord be with you all.*
  ~ II Thessalonians 3:16
- *You will keep him in perfect peace, whose mind is stayed on You, because he trusts in You.*
  ~ Isaiah 26:3
- *And let the peace of God rule in your hearts, to which also you were called in one body; and be thankful.*
  ~ Colossians 3:15

You made it to day 21! In this last devotional day, I want to encourage you that it's God's will that you live in His supernatural peace. Peace is the fruit of the Holy Spirit in your life. Fruit takes time to cultivate and grow. With patience, you will reap a magnificent harvest of the peace that passes all understanding.

I want to recap and codify the main points to maintaining supernatural peace in your life. I do not like complicated. I like things straight to the point and legible. Let's not fog things up with a theological language and psychological babble. The Bible was never meant to only be interpreted by some intellectual scholar.

> *At that time Jesus prayed this prayer: "O Father, Lord of heaven and earth, thank you for hiding these things from those who think themselves wise and clever, and for revealing them to the childlike."*
> *~ Matthew 11:25 NLT*

1) **Trust and obey:** The highest level of faith is to trust when you cannot see or understand. Always obey and do what's right no matter the opposition. Choosing the right thing will always be the right thing.

> *⁵Trust in the Lord with all your heart, and lean not on your own understanding; ⁶In all your ways acknowledge Him, and He shall direct your paths.*
> *~ Proverbs 3:5-6*

2) **Pray through to God's peace:** Pray in tongues often. Learn to give yourself to praying in your supernatural, heavenly language. Pray until anxiety lifts.

> *⁶Be anxious for nothing, but in everything by prayer and supplication, with thanksgiving, let your requests be made known to God; ⁷and the peace of God, which surpasses all understanding, will guard your hearts and minds through Christ Jesus.*
> *~ Philippians 4:6-7*

3) **Be led by the peace of God:** As we grow in our faith, we learn to discern the peace of God. If you listen to your heart, you will hear where God's peace is leading you. It may not be the easy way, but it will always be the best way. The peace of God will be the umpire of your heart.

And let the peace of God rule in your hearts, to which also
you were called in one body; and be thankful.
~ Colossians 3:15

4) Do everything you can to be at peace with others without compromising the truth of the Word of God:

If it is possible, as much as depends on you,
live peaceably with all men.
~ Romans 12:18

These are the main points of this devotional. They are presented in many different ways, but this is the bottom line: having peace with God and man is the ideal. Having peace with man is by far the hardest, but even in conflict, we can reach for, and achieve, God's peace and assurance.

I want to pray for you, my friend:

Dear God,
You know how much we love and appreciate You.
We can never put into words or repay all that You
have done, and will do, for us. I lift the reader of this
devotional up to You. I pray for Your keeping power over
their life. I pray that You bless them and keep them in
Your peace, joy, and hope. I pray that they would so
abound in these things that the world would take notice.
Fill them NOW with Your supernatural peace. Help them
to work these principles and walk in tremendous victory.
In the mighty and precious name of Jesus, King of Kings
and Lord of Lords. Amen

CPSIA information can be obtained
at www.ICGtesting.com
Printed in the USA
BVHW092307230221
600896BV00009B/1342